Thirty-three Stata Tips

Thirty-three Stata Tips

A Stata Press Publication
StataCorp LP
College Station, Texas

Stata Press, 4905 Lakeway Drive, College Station, Texas 77845

Contents

Editors' Preface

The booklet you are reading reprints 33 Stata Tips from the *Stata Journal*, with thanks to their original authors. We, the *Journal* editors, began publishing tips in 2003, beginning with volume 3, issue 4. It pleases us now to introduce them in this booklet.

The *Stata Journal* publishes substantive and peer-reviewed articles ranging from reports of original work to tutorials on statistical methods and models implemented in Stata, and indeed on Stata itself. The original material we have published since 2001 includes special issues such as those on measurement error models (volume 3, number 4, 2003) and simulated maximum likelihood (volume 6, number 2, 2006).

Other features include regular columns on Stata (currently, "Speaking Stata" and "Mata Matters"), book reviews, and announcements of software updates.

We are pleased by the external recognition that the *Journal* has achieved. In 2005, it was added to two of Thomson Scientific's citation indexes, the Science Citation Index Expanded and the CompuMath Citation Index.

But back to Tips. There was little need for tips in the early days. Stata 1.0 was released in 1985. The original program had 44 commands and its documentation totaled 175 pages. Stata 9, on the other hand, has more than 700 commands—including an embedded matrix language called Mata—and Stata's official documentation now totals more than 6,500 pages. Beyond that, the user community has added several hundred more commands.

The pluses and the minuses of this growth are evident. As Stata expands, it is increasingly likely that users' needs can be met by available code. But at the same time, learning how to use Stata and even learning what is available become larger and larger tasks.

Tips are intended to help. The ground rules for Stata Tips, as found in the original 2003 statement, are laid out as the next item in this booklet.

The Tips grew from many discussions and postings on Statalist, at Users Group meetings and elsewhere, which underscore a simple fact: Stata is now so big that it is easy to miss even simple features that can streamline and enhance your sessions with Stata. This applies not just to new users, who understandably may quake nervously before the manual mountain, but also to longtime users, who too are faced with a mass of new features in every release.

Tips have come from Stata users as well as StataCorp employees. Many discuss new features of Stata, or features not documented fully or even at all. We hope that you enjoy the Tips reprinted here and can share them with your fellow Stata users. If you have tips that you would like to write, or comments on the kinds of tips that are helpful, do get in touch with us, as we are eager to continue the series.

H. Joseph Newton, Editor
Nicholas J. Cox, Editor

The Stata Journal (2003)
3, Number 4 , p. 328

Introducing Stata tips

As promised in our editorial in *Stata Journal* 3(2), 105–108 (2003), the *Stata Journal* is hereby starting a regular column of tips. Stata tips will be a series of concise notes about Stata commands, features, or tricks that you may not yet have encountered.

The examples in this issue should indicate the kinds of tips we will publish. What we most hope for is that readers are left feeling, "I wish I'd known that earlier!" Beyond that, here are some more precise guidelines:

Content A tip will draw attention to useful details in Stata or in the use of Stata. We are especially keen to publish tips of practical value to a wide range of users. A tip could concern statistics, data management, graphics, or any other use of Stata. It may include advice on the user interface or about interacting with the operating system. Tips may explain pitfalls (don't do this) as well as positive features (do use this). Tips will not include plugs for user-written programs, however smart or useful.

Length Tips must be brief. A tip will take up at most three printed pages. Often a code example will explain just as much as a verbal discussion.

Authorship We welcome submissions of tips from readers. We also welcome suggestions of tips or of kinds of tips you would like to see, even if you do not feel that you are the person to write them. Naturally, we also welcome feedback on what has been published. An email to *editors@stata-journal.com* will reach us both.

H. Joseph Newton, Editor
Texas A&M University
jnewton@stat.tamu.edu

Nicholas J. Cox, Editor
University of Durham
n.j.cox@durham.ac.uk

Stata tip 1: The eform() option of regress

Roger Newson, King's College London, UK
roger.newson@kcl.ac.uk

Did you know about the `eform()` option of `regress`? It is very useful for calculating confidence intervals for geometric means and their ratios. These are frequently used with skewed Y-variables, such as house prices and serum viral loads in HIV patients, as approximations for medians and their ratios. In Stata, I usually do this by using the `regress` command on the logs of the Y-values, with the `eform()` and `noconstant` options. For instance, in the `auto` dataset, we might compare prices between non-US and US cars as follows:

```
. sysuse auto, clear
(1978 Automobile Data)
. generate logprice = log(price)
. generate byte baseline = 1
. regress logprice foreign baseline, noconstant eform(GM/Ratio) robust
Regression with robust standard errors        Number of obs =      74
                                               F(  2,    72) =18043.56
                                               Prob > F      =  0.0000
                                               R-squared     =  0.9980
                                               Root MSE      =  .39332
```

logprice	GM/Ratio	Robust Std. Err.	t	P>|t|	[95% Conf. Interval]	
foreign	1.07697	.103165	0.77	0.441	.8897576	1.303573
baseline	5533.565	310.8747	153.41	0.000	4947.289	6189.316

We see from the `baseline` parameter that US-made cars had a geometric mean price of 5534 dollars (95% CI from 4947 to 6189 dollars), and we see from the `foreign` parameter that non-US cars were 108% as expensive (95% CI, 89% to 130% as expensive). An important point is that, if you want to see the baseline geometric mean, then you must define the constant variable, here `baseline`, and enter it into the model with the `noconstant` option. Stata usually suppresses the display of the intercept when we specify the `eform()` option, and this trick will fool Stata into thinking that there is no intercept for it to hide. The same trick can be used with `logit` using the `or` option, if you want to see the baseline odds as well as the odds ratios.

My nonstatistical colleagues understand regression models for log-transformed data a lot better this way than any other way. Continuous X-variables can also be included, in which case the parameter for each X-variable is a ratio of Y-values per unit change in X, assuming an exponential relationship—or assuming a power relationship, if X is itself log-transformed.

The Stata Journal (2003)
3, Number 4 , pp. 446–447

Stata tip 2: Building with floors and ceilings

Nicholas J. Cox, University of Durham, UK
n.j.cox@durham.ac.uk

Did you know about the `floor()` and `ceil()` functions added in Stata 8?

Suppose that you want to round down in multiples of some fixed number. For concreteness, say, you want to round `mpg` in the auto data in multiples of 5 so that any values 10–14 get rounded to 10, any values 15–19 to 15, etc. `mpg` is simple, in that only integer values occur; in many other cases, we clearly have fractional parts to think about as well.

Here is an easy solution: `5 * floor(mpg/5)`. `floor()` always rounds down to the integer less than or equal to its argument. The name floor is due to Iverson (1962), the principal architect of APL, who also suggested the expressive $\lfloor x \rfloor$ notation. For further discussion, see Knuth (1997, 39) or Graham, Knuth, and Patashnik (1994, chapter 3).

As it happens, `5 * int(mpg/5)` gives exactly the same result for `mpg` in the auto data, but in general, whenever variables may be negative as well as positive, *interval* * `floor(`*expression/interval*`)` gives a more consistent classification.

Let us compare this briefly with other possible solutions. `round(mpg, 5)` is different, as this rounds to the nearest multiple of 5, which could be either rounding up or rounding down. `round(mpg - 2.5, 5)` should be fine but is also a little too much like a dodge.

With `recode()`, you need two dodges, say, `-recode(-mpg,-40,-35,-30,-25,-20, -15,-10)`. Note all the negative signs; negating and then negating to reverse it are necessary because `recode()` uses its numeric arguments as upper limits; i.e., it rounds up.

`egen, cut()` offers another solution with option call `at(10(5)45)`. Being able to specify a *numlist* is nice, as compared with spelling out a comma-separated list, but you *must* also add a limit, here 45, which will not be used; otherwise, with `at(10(5)40)`, your highest class will be missing.

Yutaka Aoki also suggested to me `mpg - mod(mpg,5)`, which follows immediately once you see that rounding down amounts to subtracting the appropriate remainder. `mod(,)`, however, does not offer a correspondingly neat way of rounding up.

The `floor` solution grows on one, and it has the merit that you do not need to spell out all the possible end values, with the risk of forgetting or mistyping some. Conversely, `recode()` and `egen, cut()` are not restricted to rounding in equal intervals and remain useful for more complicated problems.

Without recapitulating the whole argument insofar as it applies to rounding up, `floor()`'s sibling `ceil()` (short for ceiling) gives a nice way of rounding up in equal intervals and is easier to work with than expressions based on `int()`.

References

Graham, R. L., D. E. Knuth, and O. Patashnik. 1994. *Concrete Mathematics: A Foundation for Computer Science.* Reading, MA: Addison–Wesley.

Iverson, K. E. 1962. *A Programming Language.* New York: Wiley.

Knuth, D. E. 1997. *The Art of Computer Programming. Volume I: Fundamental Algorithms.* Reading, MA: Addison–Wesley.

The Stata Journal (2003)
3, Number 4 , p. 448

Stata tip 3: How to be assertive

William Gould, StataCorp
wgould@stata.com

`assert` verifies the truth of a claim:

```
. assert sex=="m" | sex=="f"
. assert age>=18 & age<=65
22 contradictions in 2740 observations
assertion is false
r(9);
```

The best feature of `assert` is that, when the claim is false, it stops do-files and ado-files:

```
. do my_data_prep
. use basedata, clear
. assert age>=18 & age<=64
22 contradictions in 2740 observations
assertion is false
r(9);

end of do-file
r(9);
```

`assert` has two main uses:

1. It checks that claims made to you and suppositions you have made about the data you are about to process are true:

   ```
   . assert exp==. if age<18
   . assert exp<. if age>=18
   ```

2. It tests that, when you write complicated code, the code produces what you expect:

   ```
   . sort group
   . by group: gen avg = sum(hours)/sum(hours<.)
   . by group: assert avg!=. if _n==_N
   . by group: gen relative = hours/avg[_N]
   ```

`assert` is especially useful following `merge`:

```
. merge id
. sort id using demog
. assert _merge==3
. drop _merge
```

The Stata Journal (2004)
4, Number 1 , p. 93

Stata tip 4: Using display as an online calculator

Philip Ryan, University of Adelaide
philip.ryan@adelaide.edu.au

Do you use Stata for your data management, graphics, and statistical analysis but switch to a separate device for quick calculations? If so, you might consider the advantages of using Stata's built-in `display` command:

1. It is always at hand on your computer.

2. As with all Stata calculations, double precision is used.

3. You can specify the format of results.

4. It uses and reinforces your grasp of Stata's full set of built-in functions.

5. You can keep an audit trail of results and the operations that produced those results, as part of a log file. You can also add extra comments to the output.

6. Editing of complex expressions is easy, without having to re-enter lengthy expressions after a typo.

7. You can copy and paste results elsewhere whenever your platform supports that.

8. It is available via the menu interface (select **Data—Other utilities—Hand calculator**).

9. It can be abbreviated to `di`.

To be fair, there are some disadvantages, such as its lack of support for Reverse Polish Notation or complex number arithmetic, but in total, `display` provides you with a powerful but easy-to-use calculator.

```
. di _pi
3.1415927
. di %12.10f _pi
3.1415926536
. * probability of 2 heads in 6 tosses of a fair coin
. di comb(6,2) * 0.5^2 * 0.5^4
.234375
. di "chi-square (1 df) cutting off 5% in upper tail is " invchi2tail(1, .05)
chi-square (1 df) cutting off 5% in upper tail is 3.8414588
. * Euler-Mascheroni gamma
. di %12.10f -digamma(1)
0.5772156649
```

The Stata Journal (2004)
4, Number 1 , p. 94

Stata tip 5: Ensuring programs preserve dataset sort order

Roger Newson, King's College London, UK
roger.newson@kcl.ac.uk

Did you know about `sortpreserve`? If you are writing a Stata program that temporarily changes the order of the data and you want the data to be sorted in its original order at the end of execution, you can save a bit of programming by including `sortpreserve` on your `program` statement. If your program is called `myprogram`, you can start it with

```
program myprogram, sortpreserve
```

If you do this, you can change the order of observations in the dataset in `myprogram`, and Stata will automatically sort it in its original order at the end of execution. Stata does this by creating a temporary variable whose name is stored in a macro named `_sortindex`, which is discussed in the manuals under [P] **sortpreserve**. (Note, however, that there is a typo in the manual; the underscore in `_sortindex` is missing.) The temporary variable '`_sortindex`' contains the original sort order of the data, and the dataset is sorted automatically by '`_sortindex`' at the end of the program's execution.

If you know about temporary variables, you might think that `sortpreserve` is unnecessary because you can always include two lines at the beginning, such as

```
tempvar order
generate long 'order' = _n
```

and a single line at the end such as

```
sort 'order'
```

and do the job of `sortpreserve` in 3 lines. However, `sortpreserve` does more than that. It restores the result of the macro extended function `sortedby` to the value that it would have had before your program executed. (See [P] **macro** for a description of `sortedby`.) Also, it restores the "`Sorted by:`" variable list reported by the `describe` command to the variable list that would have been reported before your program executed. For example, in the `auto` dataset shipped with official Stata, the output of `describe` ends with the message

```
Sorted by:  foreign
```

This will not be changed if you execute a program defined with `sortpreserve`.

The Stata Journal (2004)
4, Number 1 , pp. 95–96

Stata tip 6: Inserting awkward characters in the plot

Nicholas J. Cox, University of Durham, UK
n.j.cox@durham.ac.uk

Did you know about the function `char()`? `char`(n) returns the character corresponding to ASCII code n for $1 \leq n \leq 255$. There are several numbering schemes for so-called ASCII characters. Stata uses the ANSI scheme; a web search for "ANSI character set" will produce tables showing available characters. This may sound like an arcane programmer's tool, but it offers a way to use awkward text characters—either those not available through your keyboard or those otherwise problematic in Stata. A key proviso, however, is that you must have such characters available in the font that you intend to use. Fonts available tend to vary not only with platform but even down to what is installed on your own system. Some good fonts for graphics, in particular, are Arial and Times New Roman.

Let us see how this works by considering the problem of inserting awkward characters in your Stata graphs, say as part of some plot or axis title. Some examples of possibly useful characters are

`char(133)`	ellipsis	$\ldots$
`char(134)`	dagger	†
`char(135)`	double dagger	‡
`char(169)`	copyright	©
`char(176)`	degree symbol	°
`char(177)`	plus or minus	±
`char(178)`	superscript 2	^{2}
`char(179)`	superscript 3	^{3}
`char(181)`	micro symbol	μ
`char(188)`	one-fourth	$\frac{1}{4}$
`char(189)`	one-half	$\frac{1}{2}$
`char(190)`	three-fourths	$\frac{3}{4}$
`char(215)`	multiply	$\times$

There are many others that might be useful to you, including a large selection of accented letters of the alphabet. You can use such characters indirectly or directly. The indirect way is to place such characters in a local macro and then to refer to that macro within the same program or do-file.

For example, I use data on river discharge, for which the standard units are cubic meters per second. I can get the cube power in an axis title like this:

```
. local cube = char(179)
. scatter whatever, xtitle("discharge, m`cube'/s")
```

Or, I have used Hanning, a binomial filter of length 3:

```
. local half = char(189)
. local quarter = char(188)
. twoway connected whatever,
>         title("Smoothing with weights `quarter':`half':`quarter'")
```

The direct way is to get a macro evaluation on the fly. You can write '=char(176)' and, in one step, get the degree symbol (for temperatures or compass bearings). This feature was introduced in Stata 7 but not documented until Stata 8. See [P] **macro**.

char() has many other uses besides graphs. Suppose that a string variable contains fields separated by tabs. For example, insheet leaves tabs unchanged. Knowing that a tab is char(9), we can

```
. split data, p(`=char(9)') destring
```

Note that p(char(9)) would not work. The argument to the parse() option is taken literally, but the function is evaluated on the fly as part of macro substitution.

Note also that the SMCL directive {c #} may be used for some but not all of these purposes. See [P] **smcl**. Thus,

```
. scatter whatever, xtitle("discharge, m{c 179}/s")
```

would work, but using a SMCL directive would not work as desired with split.

The Stata Journal (2004)
4, Number 2 , p. 220

Stata tip 7: Copying and pasting under Windows

Shannon Driver
StataCorp
sdriver@stata.com

Patrick Royston
MRC Clinical Trials Unit, London
patrick.royston@ctu.mrc.ac.uk

Windows users often copy, cut, and paste material between applications or between windows within applications. Here are two ways you can do this with Stata for Windows. We will describe one as a mouse-and-keyboard operation and the other as a menu-based operation. Experienced Windows users will know that these methods are, to a large extent, alternatives.

First, you can highlight some text in the Results window, copy it using the mouse (or keyboard), and then paste it into the Command window, the Do-file Editor, or anywhere else appropriate. This is a convenient way to transfer, for example, single values, lists, or sets of variable names from the screen for use in the next command. To copy text, place your mouse at the beginning of the desired text, drag to the end, thus highlighting the selected text, and press Ctrl-C. To paste text, click your mouse at the appropriate place and press Ctrl-V.

Suppose that a local macro 'macro' holds some text you wish to use. Then type

```
. display "'macro'"
```

and copy and paste the contents of 'macro' for editing in the Command window. Or, list in alphabetic order the names of variables not beginning with _I:

```
. ds _I*, not alpha
```

and then copy and paste the list into the Do-file Editor.

Second, suppose that you want to save a table constructed using tabstat in a form that makes it easy to convert into a table in MS Word. Stata has a **Copy Table** feature that you might find very useful. Make sure at the outset that you have set suitable options by clicking **Edit** in the menu bar and then **Table Copy Options**. In this case, removing all the vertical bars is advisable, so make sure **Remove all** is selected, and click **OK**. Now highlight the table in the Results window, and then click **Edit** and then **Copy Table**.

In MS Word, click **Edit** and then **Paste**. Highlight the pasted text and then click **Table** and then **Convert** and **Text to Table**. Specify **Tabs** under the **Separate text at** if it is not already selected. Click **OK** to create your table.

The Stata Journal (2004)
4, Number 2 , pp. 221–222

Stata tip 8: Splitting time-span records with categorical time-varying covariates

Ben Jann, ETH Zürich, Switzerland
jann@soz.gess.ethz.ch

In survival analysis, time-varying covariates are often handled by the method of episode splitting. The stsplit command does this procedure very well, especially in the case of continuous time-varying variables such as age or time in study. Quite often, however, we are interested in evaluating the effect of a change in some kind of categorical status or the occurrence of some secondary event. For example, we might be interested in the effect of the birth of a child on the risk of divorce or the effect of having completed further education on the chances of upward occupational mobility.

In such situations, the creation of splits might appear to be more complicated, and stsplit does not seem to be of much help, at least judging from the rather complicated examples provided with [ST] **stset** (*Final example: Stanford heart transplant data*) and [ST] **stsplit** (*Example 3: Explanatory variables that change with time*). Fortunately, the procedure is simpler than it appears.

Consider the Stanford heart transplant data used in examples for [ST] **stset** and [ST] **stsplit**:

```
. use http://www.stata-press.com/data/r8/stanford, clear
(Heart transplant data)
. list id transplant wait stime died if id==44 | id==16
```

	id	transp~t	wait	stime	died
33.	44	0	0	40	1
34.	16	1	20	43	1

The goal here is to split the single time-span records into episodes before and after transplantation (e.g., to split case 16 at time 20). This can easily be achieved by splitting "at 0" "after wait", the time of transplantation. Note that, if no transplantation was carried out at all, wait should be recoded to a value larger than the observed maximum episode duration (maximum of stime) before the stsplit command is applied:

```
. replace wait = 10000 if wait == 0
(34 real changes made)
. stset stime, failure(died) id(id)
  (output omitted )
. stsplit posttran, after(wait) at(0)
(69 observations (episodes) created)
. replace posttran = posttran + 1
(172 real changes made)
```

```
. list id _t0 _t posttran if id == 44 | id == 16
```

	id	_t0	_t	posttran
23.	16	0	20	0
24.	16	20	43	1
70.	44	0	40	0

It is now possible to evaluate the effect of transplantation on survival time using
streg, for example, or to plot survivor functions with time-dependent group member-
ship:

```
. sts graph, by(posttran)
        failure _d: died
  analysis time _t: stime
              id: id
```

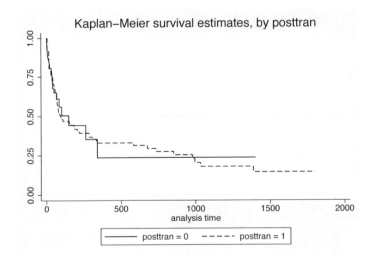

Note that the situation is even simpler if a Cox proportional hazards model is to
be fitted. As explained in [ST] **stsplit**, the partial likelihood estimator takes only the
times at which failures occur into account. Thus, in the context of Cox regression, the
following code would do:

```
. use http://www.stata-press.com/data/r8/stanford, clear
. stset stime, failure(died) id(id)
. stsplit, at(failures)
. generate posttran = wait<_t & wait!=0
. stjoin
. stcox age posttran surgery year
```

The Stata Journal (2004)
4, Number 2 , p. 223

Stata tip 9: Following special sequences

Nicholas J. Cox
University of Durham, UK
n.j.cox@durham.ac.uk

Did you know about the special sequences stored as c-class values? [P] **creturn** documents various constant and current values, which may be seen by `creturn list` or which may be accessed once you know their individual names. For example, `c(filename)` stores the name of the file last specified with a `use` or `save` in the current session. However, various special sequences have been added in updates on 1 July 2003 and 15 December 2003 and so are not documented in the manuals. Here is the list:

- `c(alpha)` returns a string containing a space-separated list of the lowercase letters.

- `c(ALPHA)` returns a string containing a space-separated list of the uppercase letters.

- `c(Mons)` returns a string containing a space-separated list of month names abbreviated to three characters.

- `c(Months)` returns a string containing a space-separated list of month names.

- `c(Wdays)` returns a string containing a space-separated list of weekday names abbreviated to three characters.

- `c(Weekdays)` returns a string containing a space-separated list of weekday names.

Even the display of one of these lists can be useful. Note the local macro notation ' ' ensuring that the contents of the list are shown, not its name:

```
. display "`c(Months)'"
```

A common application of these lists is specifying variable or value labels. Suppose that a variable `month` included values 1 to 12. We might type

```
. tokenize `c(Months)'
. forvalues i = 1/12 {
  2. label def month `i' "``i''" , modify
  3. }
. label val month month
```

Finally, the SSC archive (see [R] **ssc**) is organized alphabetically using folders `a` through `z` and `_`. We could get a complete listing of what was available by

```
. foreach l in `c(alpha)' _ {
  2. ssc describe `l'
  3. }
```

The Stata Journal (2004)
4, Number 3 , pp. 354–355

Stata tip 10: Fine control of axis title positions

Philip Ryan
University of Adelaide
philip.ryan@adelaide.edu.au

Nicholas Winter
Cornell University
nw53@cornell.edu

ytitle(), xtitle(), and other similar options specify the titles that appear on the axes of Stata graphs (see [G] *axis_title_options*). Usually, Stata's default settings produce titles with a satisfactory format and position relative to the axis. Sometimes, however, you will need finer control over position, especially if there is inadequate separation of the title and the numeric axis labels. This might happen, for example, with certain combinations of the font of the axis labels, the angle the labels make with the axis, the length of the labels, and the size of the graph region.

Although the options ylabel() and xlabel() have a suboption labgap() allowing user control of the gap between tick marks and labels (see [G] *axis_label_options*), the axis title options have no such suboption. The flexibility needed is provided by options controlling the textbox that surrounds the axis title (see [G] *textbox_options*). This box is invisible by default but can be displayed using the box suboption on the axis title option:

```
. graph twoway scatter price weight,
        ytitle("Price of Cars in {c S|}US", box)
        ylab(0(1000)15000, angle(horizontal) labsize(medium))
```

(Note the use of a SMCL directive to render the dollar sign; see [P] **smcl**, page 393.) We can manipulate the relative size of the height of the textbox or the margins around the text within the box to induce the appearance of a larger or smaller gap between the axis title and the axis labels. For a larger gap, we might try one of these solutions:

```
. graph twoway scatter price weight,
        ytitle("Price of Cars in {c S|}US", height(10))
        ylab(0(1000)15000, ang(hor) labsize(medium))
. graph twoway scatter price weight,
        ytitle("Price of Cars in {c S|}US", margin(0 10 0 0))
        ylab(0(1000)15000, ang(hor) labsize(medium))
```

For a smaller gap, specify negative arguments, say, height(-1) in the first command or margin(0 -4 0 0) in the second. A bit of trial and error will quickly give a satisfactory result.

Note that a sufficiently large negative argument in either height() or margin() will permit an axis title to be placed within the inner plot region, namely, inside of the axis. However, this, in turn, may cause the axis labels to disappear off the graph, so that some fiddling with the graphregion() option and its own margin() suboption may then be required (see [G] *region_options* and [G] *marginstyle*). For example,

```
. graph twoway scatter price weight,
        ytitle("Price of Cars in {c S|}US", height(-20))
        ylab(0(1000)15000, ang(hor) labsize(medium))
```

```
. graph twoway scatter price weight,
      ytitle("Price of Cars in {c S|}US", height(-20))
      ylab(0(1000)15000, ang(hor) labsize(medium))
      graphregion(margin(l+20))
```

margin() allows more flexibility in axis title positioning than does height(), but the price is a slightly more complicated syntax. For example, the y axis title may be moved farther from the axis labels and closer to the top of the graph by specifying both the right-hand margin and the bottom margin of the text within the box:

```
. graph twoway scatter price weight,
      ytitle("Price of Cars in {c S|}US", margin(0 10 40 0))
      ylab(0(1000)15000, ang(hor) labsize(medium))
```

The Stata Journal (2004)
4, Number 3 , p. 356

Stata tip 11: The nolog option with maximum-likelihood modeling commands

Patrick Royston
MRC Clinical Trials Unit, London
patrick.royston@ctu.mrc.ac.uk

Many Stata commands fit a model by maximum likelihood, and in so doing, they include a report on the iterations of the algorithm towards (it is hoped) eventual convergence. There may be tens or even hundreds or thousands of such lines in a report, which are faithfully recorded in any log file you may have open. Suppose that you did this with `stcox`:

```
. use http://www.stata-press.com/data/r8/cancer, clear
. describe
. stset studytime, failure(died)
. xi: stcox i.drug age, nohr
```

You get six useless lines of output detailing the progress of the algorithm. This is a nice example, as sometimes progress is much slower or more complicated.

Those lines are of little or no statistical interest in most examples and may be omitted by adding the `nolog` option:

```
. xi: stcox i.drug age, nohr nolog
```

The `nolog` option works with many vital Stata commands, including `glm`, `logistic`, `streg`, and several more. My own view is that `nolog` should be the default in all of them. Be that as it may, you can compress your logs to good effect by specifying `nolog` routinely. It will remain obvious when your estimation fails to converge.

The Stata Journal (2004)
4, Number 3 , pp. 357–358

Stata tip 12: Tuning the plot region aspect ratio

Nicholas J. Cox
University of Durham, UK
n.j.cox@durham.ac.uk

Sometimes you want a graph to have a particular shape. Graph shape is customarily quantified by the aspect ratio (height/width). One standard way of controlling the aspect ratio is setting the graph height and width by specifying the `ysize()` and `xsize()` options of `graph display`. See also [G] **graph display** and [G] *region_options*. These options control the size and, thus, the shape of the entire available graph area, including titles and other stuff beyond the plot region. At best, this is an indirect way of controlling the plot region shape, which is likely to be your main concern.

In the 23 July 2004 update, Stata 8 added an `aspect()` option to `graph` to meet this need. For example, `aspect(1)` specifies equal height and width, so that the rectangular plot region becomes a square. (A rectangle that is not a square is, strictly, an oblong.) You might want a square plot as a matter either of logic or of taste. Suppose that you are contemplating uniform random numbers falling like raindrops on the unit square within the real plane (or the plain, or as the old song has it):

```
. clear
. set obs 100
. gen y = uniform()
. gen x = uniform()
. scatter y x, aspect(1) xla(0(0.1)1, grid) yla(0(0.1)1, ang(h) grid)
> yti(, orient(horiz)) plotregion(margin(none))
```

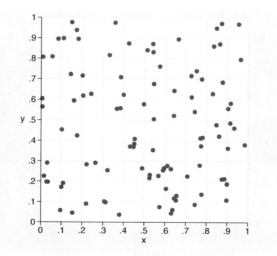

In effect you have drawn a map, and maps customarily have equal vertical and horizontal distance scales or, more simply put, a single distance scale. Hence the aspect ratio is set as 1 whenever the plot region has equal extent on both axes. The same preference applies also to various special graphs on the unit square, such as ROC or Lorenz curves.

In other circumstances, the aspect ratio sought might differ from 1. Fisher (1925, 31) recommended plotting data so that lines make approximately equal angles with both axes; the same advice of banking to 45° is discussed in much more detail by Cleveland (1993). Avoiding roller-coaster plots of time series is one application. In practice, a little trial and error will be needed to balance a desire for equal angles with other considerations. For example, try variations on the following:

```
. use http://www.stata-press.com/data/r8/htourism.dta
. tsline mvdays, aspect(0.15) yla(, ang(h))
```

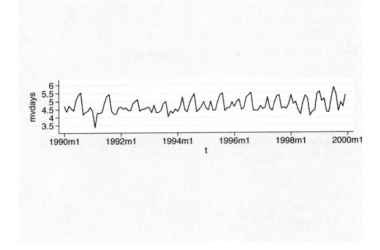

References

Cleveland, W. S. 1993. *Visualizing Data*. Summit, NJ: Hobart Press.

Fisher, R. A. 1925. *Statistical Methods for Research Workers*. Edinburgh: Oliver & Boyd.

The Stata Journal (2004)
4, Number 4 , pp. 484–485

Stata tip 13: generate and replace use the current sort order

Roger Newson
King's College London, UK
roger.newson@kcl.ac.uk

Did you know that `generate` and `replace` use the current sort order? You might have guessed this because otherwise the `sum()` function could work as designed only with difficulty. However, this fact is not documented in the manuals, but only in the Stata web site FAQs. The consequence is that, given a particular desired `sort` order, you can be sure that values of a variable are calculated in that order and can use them to calculate subsequent values of the same variable.

A simple example is filling in missing values by copying the previous nonmissing value. The syntax for this is simply

```
. replace myvar = myvar[_n-1] if missing(myvar)
```

Here the subscript `[_n-1]`, based on the built-in variable `_n`, refers to the previous observation in the present sort order. To find more about subscripts, see [U] **13.7 Explicit subscripting** or the online help for `subscripting`.

Suppose that values of `myvar` are present for observations 1, 2, and 5 but missing in observations 3, 4, and 6. `replace` starts by replacing `myvar[3]` with the nonmissing `myvar[2]`. It then replaces `myvar[4]` with `myvar[3]`, which now contains (just in time) a copy of the nonmissing `myvar[2]`. Finally, `replace` puts a copy of `myvar[5]` into `myvar[6]`. As said, this all requires that data are in the desired sort order, commonly that of some time variable. If not, reach for the `sort` command.

There are numerous variations on this idea. Suppose that a sequence of years contains nonmissing values only for years like 1980, 1990, and 2000. This is common in data derived from spreadsheet files. A simple fix would be

```
. replace year = year[_n-1] + 1 if mi(year)
```

That way, changes cascade down the observations.

More exotic examples concern recurrence relations, as found in probability theory and elsewhere in mathematics. We typically use `generate` to define the first value (or the first few values) and `replace` to define the other values.

Consider the famous "birthday problem": what is the probability that no two out of n people have the same birthday? Assuming equal probabilities of birth on each of 365 days, and so ignoring leap years and seasonal fertility variation, this probability is $\prod_{j=1}^{n} x_j$, where $x_j = (365 - j + 1)/365$. We can put these probabilities into a variable `palldiff` by typing

```
. set obs 370
. generate double palldiff = 1
. replace palldiff = palldiff[_n-1] * (365 - _n + 1) / 365 in 2/l
. label var palldiff "Pr(All birthdays are different)"
. list palldiff
```

To illustrate, the probability that all birthdays are different is below 0.5 for 23 people, below one-millionth for 97 people, and zero for over 365 people. An alternative solution (based on a suggestion by Roberto Gutierrez) is to replace the second and third lines of the above program with

```
. generate double palldiff = 0
. replace palldiff = exp(sum(ln(366 - _n) - ln(365))) in 1/365
```

which works because the product of positive numbers is the sum of their logarithms, exponentiated.

Another example is the Fibonacci sequence, defined by $y_1 = y_2 = 1$ and otherwise by $y_n = y_{n-1} + y_{n-2}$. The first 20 numbers are given by

```
. set obs 20
. generate y = 1
. replace y = y[_n-1] + y[_n-2] in 3/l
. list y
```

If you ever want to work backwards by referring to later observations, it is often easiest to reverse the order of observations and then to use tricks like these.

The Stata Journal (2004)
4, Number 4 , pp. 486–487

Stata tip 14: **Using value labels in expressions**

Kenneth Higbee
StataCorp
khigbee@stata.com

Did you know that there is a way in Stata to specify value labels directly in an expression, rather than through the underlying numeric value? You specify the label in double quotes (`" "`), followed by a colon (`:`), followed by the name of the value label. If we read in this dataset and see what it contains

```
. webuse census9
(1980 Census data by state)
. describe
Contains data from http://www.stata-press.com/data/r8/census9.dta
  obs:          50                          1980 Census data by state
  vars:          5                          16 Jul 2002 18:29
  size:       1,550 (99.9% of memory free)

              storage  display     value
variable name   type   format      label     variable label

state          str14   %-14s                  State
drate          float   %9.0g                  Death Rate
pop            long    %12.0gc                Population
medage         float   %9.2f                  Median age
region         byte    %-8.0g      cenreg     Census region

Sorted by:
```

we notice that variable `region` has values labeled by the `cenreg` value label. The correspondence between the underlying number and the value label is shown by

```
. label list
cenreg:
          1 NE
          2 N Cntrl
          3 South
          4 West
```

[R] **regress** uses this dataset to illustrate weighted regression. To obtain the regression of `drate` and `medage` restricted to the "South" region, you could type

```
. regress drate medage [aweight=pop] if region == 3
```

But, if you do not remember the underlying region number for "South", you could also obtain this regression by typing

```
. regress drate medage [aweight=pop] if region == "South":cenreg
(sum of wgt is   7.4734e+07)
```

Source	SS	df	MS
Model	1072.30989	1	1072.30989
Residual	550.163155	14	39.2973682
Total	1622.47305	15	108.16487

```
                                        Number of obs =      16
                                        F(  1,    14) =   27.29
                                        Prob > F      =  0.0001
                                        R-squared     =  0.6609
                                        Adj R-squared =  0.6367
                                        Root MSE      =  6.2688
```

drate	Coef.	Std. Err.	t	P>|t|	[95% Conf. Interval]	
medage	3.905819	.7477109	5.22	0.000	2.302139	5.509499
_cons	-29.34031	22.33676	-1.31	0.210	-77.2479	18.56727

Typing the value label instead of the underlying number makes it unlikely that you will obtain an unintended result from entering the wrong region number. An added benefit of using the value label is that, when you later review your results, you will quickly see that the regression is for the "South" region, and you will not need to remember what region was assigned number 3.

See [U] **13.9 Label values** for further information about specifying value labels in expressions.

The Stata Journal (2004)
4, Number 4 , pp. 488–489

Stata tip 15: Function graphs on the fly

Nicholas J. Cox
University of Durham, UK
n.j.cox@durham.ac.uk

[G] **graph twoway function** gives several examples of how function graphs may be drawn on the fly. The manual entry does not quite explain the full flexibility and versatility of the command. Here is a further advertisement on its behalf. To underline a key feature: you do not need to create variables following particular functions. The command handles all of that for you. We will look at two more examples.

A common simple need is to draw a circle. A trick with `twoway function` is to draw two half-circles, upper and lower, and combine them. If you are working in some scheme using color, you will usually also want to ensure that the two halves are shown in the same color. The `aspect()` option was explained in Cox (2004).

```
. twoway function sqrt(1 - x * x), ra(-1 1) ||
>         function -sqrt(1 - x * x), ra(-1 1) aspect(1)
>         legend(off) yla(, ang(h)) ytitle(, orient(horiz)) clp(solid)
```

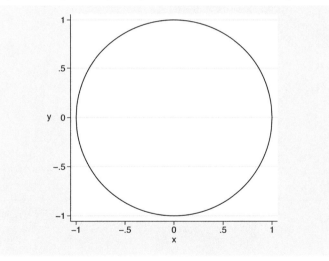

MacKay (2003, 316) asserts that, if we transform beta distributions of variables P between 0 and 1 to the corresponding densities over logit $P = \ln[P/(1 - P)]$, then we find always pleasant bell-shaped densities. In contrast, densities over P may have singularities at $P = 0$ and $P = 1$. This is the kind of textbook statement that should provoke some play with friendly statistical graphics software.

To explore MacKay's assertion, we need a standard result on changing variables (see, for example, Evans and Rosenthal 2004, theorems 2.6.2 and 2.6.3). Suppose that P is an absolutely continuous random variable with density function f_P, h is a function that is differentiable and monotone, and $X = h(P)$. The density function of X is then

$$f_X(x) = \frac{f_P\{h^{-1}(x)\}}{|h'\{h^{-1}(x)\}|}$$

In our case, $h(P) = \text{logit } P$, so that $h^{-1}(X) = \exp(X)/\{1+\exp(X)\}$ and $h'\{h^{-1}(X)\} = \{1 + \exp(X)\}^2/\exp(X)$. In Stata terms, beta densities transformed to the logit scale are the product of `betaden(p)` or `betaden(invlogit(x))` and `exp(x)/(1+exp(x))^2`. The latter term may be recognized as a logistic density function, which always has a bell shape.

An example pair of original and transformed distributions is given by the commands below. To explore further in parameter space, you need only vary the parameters from 0.5 and 0.5 (and, if desired, to vary the range).

```
. twoway function betaden(0.5,0.5,x), ytitle(density) xtitle(p)
. twoway function betaden(0.5,0.5,invlogit(x)) * (exp(x) / (1 + exp(x))^2),
> ra(-10 10) ytitle(density) xtitle(logit p)
```

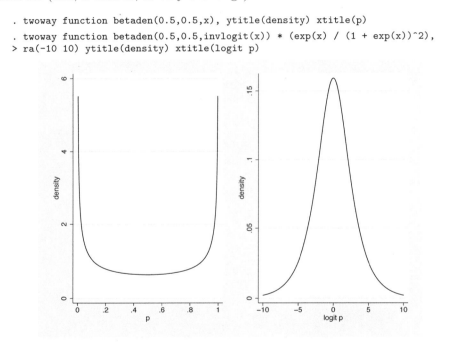

References

Cox, N. J. 2004. Stata tip 12: Tuning the plot region aspect ratio. *Stata Journal* 4: 357–358.

Evans, M. J., and J. S. Rosenthal. 2004. *Probability and Statistics: The Science of Uncertainty.* New York: W. H. Freeman.

MacKay, D. J. C. 2003. *Information Theory, Inference, and Learning Algorithms.* Cambridge: Cambridge University Press. Also available at http://www.inference.phy.cam.ac.uk/mackay/itprnn/book.html.

The Stata Journal (2005)
5, Number 1 , p. 134

Stata tip 16: Using input to generate variables

Ulrich Kohler
Wissenschaftszentrum Berlin für Sozialforschung
kohler@wz-berlin.de

Sometimes using `generate` is an untidy and long-winded way to generate new variables, particularly if the variable you want to create is categorical and there are many different categories. Thus rather than using

```
. gen iso3166_2 = "AT" if country == "Austria"
. replace iso3166_2 = "BE" if country == "Belgium"
. replace iso3166_2 = "TR" if country == "Turkey"
```
and so on for say 28 countries
```
. gen iso3166_3 = "AUT" if country == "Austria"
. replace iso3166_3 = "BEL" if country == "Belgium"
. replace iso3166_3 = "TUR" if country == "Turkey"
```
and so on for say 28 countries
```
. gen gername = "Österreich" if country == "Austria"
. replace gername = "Belgien" if country == "Belgium"
. replace gername = "Türkei" if country == "Turkey"
```
and so on for say 28 countries

you can use `input` to produce a new dataset, `save` to a temporary file, and then `merge`:

```
. preserve
. clear
. input str15 country str2 iso3166_2 str3 iso3166_3 str15 gername
 Austria AT AUT Österreich
 Belgium BE BEL Belgien
 Turkey  TK TUR Türkei
```
and so on
```
. end

. sort country
. tempfile foo
. save `foo'
. restore
. sort country
. merge country using `foo'
```

Among the benefits are less typing; a cleaner log file; in huge datasets, faster data processing; and arguably fewer errors.

See [R] **input**[1] for the finer points on `input`.

---

1. For Stata 9, see [D] **input**.

The Stata Journal (2005)
5, Number 1 , pp. 135–136

Stata tip 17: Filling in the gaps

Nicholas J. Cox
University of Durham, UK
n.j.cox@durham.ac.uk

The `fillin` command (see [R] **fillin**[1]) does precisely one thing: it fills in the gaps in a rectangular data structure. That is very well explained in the manual entry, but people who do not yet know the command often miss it, so here is one more plug. Suppose that you have a dataset of people and the choices they make, something like this:

```
id   choice
1    1
2    3
3    1
4    2
```

Now suppose that you wish to run a nested logit model using `nlogit` (see [R] **nlogit**). This command requires all choices, those made and those not made, to be explicit. With even 4 values of `id` and 3 values of `choice`, we need 12 observations so that each combination of variables exists once in the dataset; hence, 8 more are needed in this case. The solution is just

```
. fillin id choice
```

and a new variable, `_fillin`, is added to the dataset with values 1 if the observation was "filled in" and 0 otherwise. Thus `count if _fillin` tells you how many observations were added. You will often want to `replace` or `rename _fillin` to something appropriate:

```
. rename _fillin chosen
. replace chosen = 1 - chosen
```

If you do not `rename` or `drop _fillin`, it will get in the way of a subsequent `fillin`. Usually, the decision is clear-cut: Either `_fillin` has a natural interpretation, so you want to keep it, or a relative, under a different name; or `_fillin` was just a by-product, and you can get rid of it without distress.

Another common variant is to show zero counts or amounts explicitly. With a dataset of political donations for several years, we might want an observation showing that `amount` is zero for each pair of `donor` and `year` not matched by a donation. This typically leads to neater tables and graphs and may be needed for modeling: in particular, for panel models, the zeros must be present as observations. The main idea is the same, but the aftermath is different:

```
. fillin donor year
. replace amount = 0 if _fillin
```

---

1. For Stata 9, see [D] **fillin**.

Naturally if we have more than one donation from various donors in various years, we might also want to `collapse` (or just possibly `contract`) the data, but that is the opposite kind of problem.

Yet another common variant is the creation of a grid for some purpose, perhaps before data entry, or before you draw a graph. You can be very lazy by typing

```
. clear
. set obs 20
. gen y = _n
. gen x = y
. fillin y x
```

which creates a 20×20 grid. This is good, but sometimes you want something different; see functions `fill()` and `seq()` in [R] **egen**.[2]

The messiest `fillin` problems are when some of the categories you want are not present in the dataset at all. If you know a person is not one of the values of `donor`, no amount of filling in will add a set of zeros for that person. One strategy here is to add pseudo-observations so that every category occurs at least once and then to `fillin` in terms of that larger dataset. This is just a variation on the technique for creating a grid out of nothing.

As far as you can see from what is here, `fillin` just does things in place, so you need not worry about file manipulation. This is an illusion, as underneath the surface, `fillin` is firing up `cross` (see [R] **cross**[3]), which does the work using files. Thus `cross` is more fundamental. A forthcoming tip will say more.

---

2. For Stata 9, see [D] **egen**.
3. For Stata 9, see [D] **cross**.

The Stata Journal (2005)
5, Number 1 , pp. 137–138

Stata tip 18: Making keys functional

Shannon Driver
StataCorp
s.driver@stata.com

Did you know that you can create custom definitions for your *F*-keys in Stata?

F-key definitions are created via global macros. On startup, Stata sets the *F*-key defaults to

F-key	definition
F1	help
F2	#review;
F3	describe;
F7	save
F8	use

You can redefine these keys if you wish.

When a definition ends with a semicolon (;), Stata will automatically execute that command as if you typed it and pressed the Enter key; otherwise, the command is immediately entered into the command line as if you had typed it. Stata then waits for you to press the Enter key. This allows you to modify the command before it is executed.

For example, to define the *F4* key to execute the `list` command, you would type

```
. global F4 "list;"
```

The "F4" here is actually a capital `F` followed by the number 4.

The best place to create these definitions is in an ASCII text file called `profile.do`. Every time Stata is launched, it looks for `profile.do` and, if it finds it, executes all of the commands it contains. For more information, type `help profile`.

Let's say that you want to create a definition for *F4* to open a window showing the contents of a particular directory. You could do this on Windows by typing

```
. global F4 `"winexec explorer C:\data;"'
```

On a Macintosh, you could type

```
. global F4 `"!open /Applications/Stata8/Stata;"'
```

You can also create *F*-key definitions to launch your favorite text editor.

```
. global F5 `"winexec notepad;"'
```

Yet another application is programming the ` and ' keys, which Stata uses to delimit local macros. Many keyboards do not have the left- or open-quote character of this pair, so an alternative is to define an *F*-key to be that key. For symmetry, you might want another *F*-key to be the right- or close-quote character. But how do you define a replacement for a key if you do not have that key in the first place? One answer lies in Stata's `char()` function:

```
. global F4 = char(96)
. global F5 = char(180)
```

You may want to make a note that *F10* is reserved internally by Windows, so you cannot program this key. Also, not all Macintosh keyboards have *F*-keys.

For more information on this topic, please see [U] **10.2 F-keys**.

Stata tip 19: A way to leaner, faster graphs

Patrick Royston
MRC Clinical Trials Unit
p.royston@ctu.mrc.ac.uk

If you have many variables, consider doing a `preserve` of the data and `dropping` several of them before drawing a graph. This greatly speeds up production.

Take plotting fitted values from a model as an example. If there are many tied observations at each value of the predictor and therefore many replicates of the fitted values, the size of the graph file can be large, also making the plotting time large. A construction like this can save resources:

```
. preserve
. bysort x: drop if _n > 1
. line f1 f2 f3 x, sort clp(l - _) saving(graph, replace)
. restore
```

Here is another real example: with 15,156 variables and 50 observations, I wanted a `dotplot` of variable `v15155` by `v15156`. The time taken with all data present was 10.66 seconds, but with `preserve` and all irrelevant variables `dropped`, it was 0.69 seconds.

The Stata Journal (2005)
5, Number 2 , pp. 280–281

Stata tip 20: Generating histogram bin variables

David A. Harrison
ICNARC, London, UK
david.harrison@icnarc.org

Did you know about `twoway__histogram_gen`? (Note the two underscores in the first gap and only one in the second.) This command is used by `histogram` to generate the variables that are plotted. It is undocumented in the manuals but explained in the online help. The command can be used directly to save these variables, enabling more complex manipulation of histograms and production of other graphs or tables.

Consider the S&P 500 historical data that are used as an example for [R] **histogram**:

```
. use http://www.stata-press.com/data/r9/sp500
(S&P 500)
. histogram volume, percent start(4000) width(1000)
(bin=20, start=4000, width=1000)
  (output omitted)
```

To display only the central part of this histogram from 8,000 to 16,000, we could use if, but this will change the height of the bars, as data outside the range 8,000 to 16,000 will be ignored completely. To restrict the range without altering the bars, we use `twoway__histogram_gen` to save the histogram and only plot the section of interest:

```
. twoway__histogram_gen volume, percent start(4000) width(1000) gen(h x)
. twoway bar h x if inrange(x,8000,16000), barwidth(1000) bstyle(histogram)
```

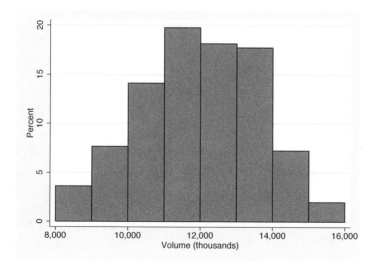

The `start()` and `width()` options above specified cutpoints that included 8,000 and 16,000. We could, alternatively, use the default cutpoints:

```
. twoway__histogram_gen volume if inrange(volume,8000,16000), display
(bin=14, start=8117, width=525.08571)
. local m = r(start)
. local w = r(width)
. summarize volume, meanonly
. local s = `m' - `w' * ceil((`m' - r(min))/`w')
. twoway__histogram_gen volume, percent start(`s') width(`w') gen(h x, replace)
. twoway bar h x if inrange(x,8000,16000), barwidth(`w') bstyle(histogram)
  (output omitted)
```

Other uses of `twoway_histogram_gen` include the following:

- Overlaying or mirroring two histograms

  ```
  . use http://www.stata-press.com/data/r9/bplong, clear
  (fictional blood-pressure data)
  . twoway__histogram_gen bp if sex == 0, frac start(125) w(5) gen(h1 x1)
  . twoway__histogram_gen bp if sex == 1, frac start(125) w(5) gen(h2 x2)
  . twoway (bar h1 x1, barw(5) bc(gs11))
  > (bar h2 x2, barw(5) blc(black) bfc(none)),
  > legend(order(1 "Male" 2 "Female"))
    (output omitted)
  . qui replace h2 = -h2
  . twoway (bar h1 x1, barw(5)) (bar h2 x2, barw(5)),
  > yla(-.2 ".2" -.1 ".1" 0 .1 .2) legend(order(1 "Male" 2 "Female"))
    (output omitted)
  ```

- Changing the scale, for example, to plot density on a square-root scale

  ```
  . twoway__histogram_gen bp, start(125) width(5) gen(h x)
  . qui gen hsqrt = sqrt(h)
  . twoway bar hsqrt x, barw(5) bstyle(histogram) ytitle(Density)
  > ylabel(0 .05 ".0025" .1 ".01" .15 ".0225" .2 ".04")
    (output omitted)
  ```

- Plotting the differences between observed and expected frequencies

  ```
  . twoway__histogram_gen bp, freq start(125) w(5) gen(h x, replace)
  . qui summarize bp
  . qui gen diff = h - r(N) * (norm((x + 2.5 - r(mean))/r(sd)) -
  > norm((x - 2.5 - r(mean))/r(sd)))
  . twoway bar diff x, barw(5) yti("Observed - expected frequency")
    (output omitted)
  ```

There are also two similar commands: `twoway_function_gen` to generate functions and `twoway_kdensity_gen` to generate kernel densities.

The Stata Journal (2005)
5, Number 2 , pp. 282–284

Stata tip 21: The arrows of outrageous fortune

Nicholas J. Cox
Durham University
n.j.cox@durham.ac.uk

Stata 9 introduces a clutch of new plottypes for `graph twoway` for paired-coordinate data. These are defined by four variables, two specifying starting coordinates and the other two specifying ending coordinates. Here we look at some of the possibilities opened up by [G] **graph twoway pcarrow** for graphing changes over time. Arrows are readily understood by novices as well as experts as indicating, in this case, the flow from the past towards the present.

Let us begin with one of the classic time-series datasets. The number of lynx trapped in an area of Canada provides an excellent example of cyclic boom-and-bust population dynamics. Trappings are optimistically assumed to be proportional to the unknown population size.

The dataset has already been `tsset` (see [TS] **tsset**).

```
. use http://www.stata-press.com/data/r9/lynx2.dta, clear
(TIMESLAB: Canadian lynx)

. tsline lynx
   (output omitted )
```

Ecologists and other statistically minded people find it natural to think about populations on a logarithmic scale: population growth is after all inherently multiplicative. Logarithms to base 10 are convenient for graphing.

(*Continued on next page*)

```
. gen loglynx = log10(lynx)
. twoway pcarrow loglynx L.loglynx F.loglynx loglynx,
> xla(2 "100" `=log10(200)' "200" `=log10(500)' "500" 3 "1000" `=log10(2000)'
> "2000" `=log10(5000)' "5000")
> yla(2 "100" `=log10(200)' "200" `=log10(500)' "500" 3 "1000" `=log10(2000)'
> "2000" `=log10(5000)' "5000")
> ytitle(this year) xtitle(previous year) subtitle(Number of lynx trapped)
```

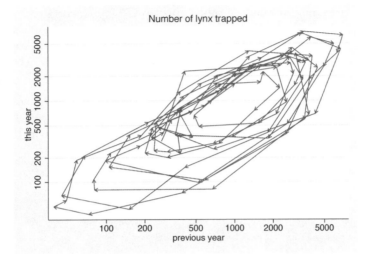

Thinking as it were autoregressively, we can plot this year's population versus the previous year's and join data points with arrows end to end. Each data point other than the first and last is the end of one arrow pointing from L.loglynx to loglynx and the beginning of another pointing from loglynx to F.loglynx. This dual role and the ability to use time-series operators such as L. and F. on the fly in graphics commands yield the command syntax just given. Plotted as a trajectory in this space, population cycles are revealed clearly as asymmetric. Depending on your background, you may see this as an example of hysteresis, or whatever else it is called in your tribal jargon.

Another basic comparison compares values for some outcome of interest at two dates. For this next example, we use life expectancy data for 1970 and 2003 from the UNICEF report, *The State of the World's Children 2005*, taken from the web site *http://www.unicef.org* accessed on May 12, 2005. A manageable graph focuses on those countries for which life expectancy was under 50 years in 2003. A count on the dataset thus entered shows that there are 33 such countries.

We borrow some ideas from displays possible with graph dot (see [G] **graph dot**). Arrows connecting pairs of variables are not supported by graph dot. However, as is common with Stata's graphics, whatever is difficult with graph dot, graph bar, or graph hbar is often straightforward with graph twoway, modulo some persistence.

A natural sort order for the graph is that of life expectancy in 2003. A nuance to make the graph tidier is to break ties according to life expectancy in 1970. Life expectancy is customarily, and sensibly, reported in integer years, so ties are common. One axis for the graph is then just the observation number given the sort order, except that we will want to name the countries concerned on the graph. For names that might be fairly long, we prefer horizontal alignment and thus a vertical axis. The names are best assigned to value labels. Looping over observations is one way to define those. The online help on `forvalues` and `macros` explains any trickery with the loop that may be unfamiliar to you; also see [P] **forvalues** and [P] **macro**.

```
. gsort lifeexp03 - lifeexp70
. gen order = _n
. forval i = 1/33 {
  2.          label def order `i' "`=country[`i']'", modify
  3. }
. label val order order
```

The main part of the graph is then obtained by a call to `twoway pcarrow`. The arrowhead denotes life expectancy in 2003. Optionally, although not essentially, we overlay a scatter plot showing the 1970 values.

```
. twoway pcarrow order lifeexp70 order lifeexp03 if lifeexp03 < 50
> || scatter order lifeexp70 if lifeexp03 < 50, ms(oh)
> yla(1/33, ang(h) notick valuelabel labsize(*0.75)) yti("") legend(off)
> barbsize(2) xtitle("Life expectancy in years, 1970 and 2003") aspect(1)
```

Apart from Afghanistan, all the countries shown are in Africa. Some show considerable improvements over this period, but in about as many, life expectancy has fallen dramatically. Readers can add their own somber commentary in terms of war, political instability, famine, and disease, particularly AIDS.

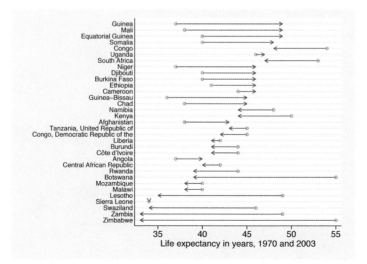

The Stata Journal (2005)
5, Number 3 , pp. 465–466

36

Stata tip 22: Variable name abbreviation

Philip Ryan
University of Adelaide
philip.ryan@adelaide.edu.au

Stata allows users to abbreviate any variable name to the shortest string of characters that uniquely identifies it, given the data currently loaded in memory (see [U] **11.2.3 Variable-name abbreviation**). Stata also offers three wildcard characters, *, ~, and ? (see [U] **11.4.1 Lists of existing variables**), so users have substantial flexibility in how variables may be referenced.

Stata also allows users to control the values of many of its system parameters using the `set` command (see [R] **set**). One of these parameters is `varabbrev`, which may be toggled on, allowing variable names to be abbreviated, or off, requiring the user to spell out entire variable names.

The default is to allow abbreviations. But this convenience feature can bite. Suppose that in a program we wish to confirm the existence of a variable and that variable does not in fact exist:

```
. clear
. set varabbrev on
. set obs 10
(obs was 0, now 10)
. generate byte myvar7 = 1
. confirm variable myvar
```

There is no error message here because `myvar` is an allowed abbreviation for `myvar7`. A bigger deal is that as `myvar7` exists and not `myvar`, typing `drop myvar` would drop `myvar7`, which may or may not have been our intention.

But what if we had wanted to confirm explicitly the existence of variable `myvar`? There are two ways to do this:

1. Specify the `confirm` command with the `exact` option (see [P] **confirm**):

   ```
   . confirm variable myvar, exact
   variable myvar not found
   r(111);
   ```

2. Toggle variable abbreviation off:

   ```
   . set varabbrev off
   . confirm variable myvar
   variable myvar not found
   r(111);
   ```

Note that the status of **varabbrev** does not affect the display of variable names. For example,

```
. sysuse auto, clear
(1978 Automobile Data)
. set varabbrev off
. rename weight this_is_a_very_long_varname
. regress price turn length this_is_a_very_long_varname
```
(*output omitted*)

price	Coef.	Std. Err.	t	P>|t|	[95% Conf. Interval]	
turn	-318.2055	127.1241	-2.50	0.015	-571.7465	-64.66452
length	-66.17856	39.87361	-1.66	0.101	-145.704	13.34684
this_is_a_~e	5.382135	1.116756	4.82	0.000	3.154834	7.609435
_cons	14967.64	4541.836	3.30	0.002	5909.228	24026.04

In this display, Stata has abbreviated the long variable name, despite the current value of **varabbrev**.

Note that the **list** command has its own option to allow the user partial control of the display; see [D] **list**. As we **set varabbrev off**, we must specify only unabbreviated variable names in a **list** command, but we can override Stata's default abbreviation in the display using the **abbreviate()** option:

```
. list make turn this_is_a_very_long_varname in 1/4, abb(21)
```

	make	turn	this_is_a_very_long~e
1.	AMC Concord	40	2,930
2.	AMC Pacer	40	3,350
3.	AMC Spirit	35	2,640
4.	Buick Century	40	3,250

The default value for **abbreviate()** is 8, so that otherwise the variable name would have been displayed as **this_i~e**.

The Stata Journal (2005)
5, Number 3 , pp. 467–468

Stata tip 23: Regaining control over axis ranges

Nicholas J. G. Winter
Cornell University
nw53@cornell.edu

Beginning with version 8, Stata will often widen the range of a graph axis beyond the range of the data. Convincing Stata to narrow the range can be difficult unless you understand the cause of the problem.

Using the trusty `auto` dataset, consider the graph produced by this command:

```
. sysuse auto, clear
(1978 Automobile Data)

. twoway scatter mpg price
```

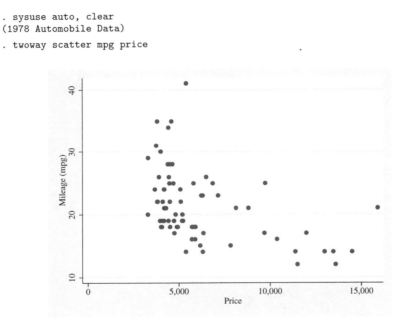

Although price ranges from $3,291 to $15,906 in the data, the lower end of the x-axis in this graph extends to zero, leaving blank space on the left-hand side. If we do not like this space, the solution would seem to lie with the `range()` suboption of the `xscale()` option. Thus we might expect Stata to range the x-axis using the minimum and maximum of the data, given the following command:

```
. twoway scatter mpg price, xscale(range(3291 15906))
```

However, this produces the same graph: the axis still includes zero. It seems that Stata is ignoring `range()`, although it does not do that when the range is *increased*, rather than decreased. Consider, for example, this command, which expands the x-axis to run from 0 through 30,000:

```
. twoway scatter mpg price, xscale(range(0 30000))
```

The issue is that the range displayed for an axis depends on the interaction between two sets of options (or their defaults): those that control the axis range explicitly, and those that *label* the axis. The range can be expanded either by explicitly specifying a longer axis (e.g., with `xscale(range(a b))`) or by labeling values outside the range of the data.

To determine the range of an axis, Stata begins with the minimum and maximum of the data. Then it will widen (but never narrow) the axis range as instructed by `range()`. Finally, it will widen the axis if necessary to accommodate any axis labels.

By default, `twoway` labels the axes with "about" five ticks, the equivalent of specifying `xlabel(#5)`. In this case, Stata chooses four labels, one of which is zero, and then expands the x-axis accordingly. In other words, if we specify `xscale()`—but do not specify `xlabel()`—we are in effect saying to Stata "and please use the default `xlabel()` for this graph". This default may widen the axis range.

Therefore, to get a narrower x-axis, we must specify a narrower set of axis labels. For example, to label just the minimum and maximum, we could specify

```
. scatter mpg price, xlabel(minmax)
```

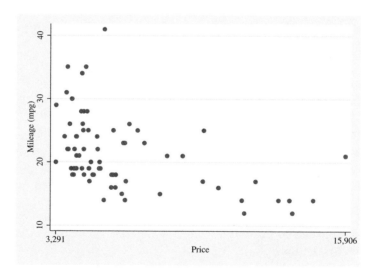

Of course, we could specify any other set of points to label, for example,

```
. scatter mpg price, xlabel(5000[1000]15000)
```

This issue only appeared with Stata version 8. Prior versions defaulted to labeling the minimum and the maximum of the data only. This would be equivalent to including the options `xlabel(minmax)` and `ylabel(minmax)` in Stata 8 or later.

The Stata Journal (2005)
5, Number 3 , p. 469

Stata tip 24: Axis labels on two or more levels

Nicholas J. Cox
Durham University
n.j.cox@durham.ac.uk

Text shown as graph axis labels is by default shown on one level. For example, a label `Foreign cars` would be shown just like that. Sometimes you want the text of a label to be shown on two or even more levels, as one way of reducing crowding or even overprinting of text; thus you might want `Foreign` written above `cars`. Other ways of fighting crowding include varying the size or angle at which text is printed (see [G] *axis_label_options* for details), or in some cases reconsidering which variable should go on which axis.

To specify multiple levels, the text to go on each level should appear within double quotes " ", and the whole text label should appear within compound double quotes ' " " '. For more explanation of the latter, see [U] **18.3.5 Double quotes**. That way, Stata's parser has a clear idea of parts and wholes.

Here are some examples:

```
. sysuse auto
. dotplot mpg, over(foreign)
> xlabel(0 '" "Domestic" "cars" "' 1 '" "Foreign" "cars" "') xtitle("")
. graph box mpg,
> over(foreign, relabel(1 '" "Domestic" "cars" "'  2 '" "Foreign" "cars" "'))
. graph hbar (mean) mpg,
> over(foreign, relabel(1 '" "Domestic" "cars" "'  2 '" "Foreign" "cars" "'))
```

Note the subtle difference between these examples. `dotplot` is really a wrapper for `twoway` and, as is characteristic of `twoway` graphs, it takes its variables literally so that the values of `foreign` are indeed treated as 0 and 1. On the other hand, graphs with so-called categorical axes (`graph bar`, `graph hbar`, `graph box`, `graph hbox`, and `graph dot`) consider the categories shown to be 1, 2, and so forth, regardless of the precise numeric or string values of the variables concerned. The numbers increase from left to right or from top to bottom, as the case may be. Thus matrix users will feel at home with this convention.

The Stata Journal (2005)
5, Number 4 , pp. 602–603

Stata tip 25: Sequence index plots

Ulrich Kohler and Christian Brzinsky-Fay
Wissenschaftszentrum Berlin
kohler@wz-berlin.de, brzinsky-fay@wz-berlin.de

Sequence index plots of longitudinal or panel data use stacked bars or line segments to show how individuals move between a set of conditions or states over time. Changes of state are shown by changes of color. The term *sequence index plot* was proposed by Brüderl and Scherer (2005, in press). See Scherer (2001) for an application.

It is possible to draw sequence index plots with Stata by using the `twoway` plottype `rbar`. Starting from data in survival-time form (see `help st`), you simply overlay separate range-bar plots for each state.

For example, suppose that you have data on times for entering and leaving various states of employment:

```
. list in 1/10
```

	id	type	begin	end
1.	1	employed	1	13
2.	1	apprenticeship	13	20
3.	1	unemployed	20	23
4.	1	employed	23	25
5.	1	unemployed	25	26
6.	1	employed	26	43
7.	1	unemployed	43	50
8.	1	employed	50	60
9.	2	employed	1	13
10.	2	apprenticeship	13	21

First, `separate` the start and end dates for the different states:

```
. separate begin, by(type)
. separate end, by(type)
```

Then plot overlaid range bars for each state:

```
. graph twoway
>    (rbar begin1 end1 id, horizontal)
>    (rbar begin2 end2 id, horizontal)
>    (rbar begin3 end3 id, horizontal)
>    (rbar begin4 end4 id, horizontal)
>    (rbar begin5 end5 id, horizontal)
>    , legend(order(1 "education" 2 "apprenticeship"
>          3 "employment" 4 "unemployment"  5 "inactivity")
>          cols(1) pos(2) symxsize(5))
>      xtitle("months") yla(, angle(h)) yscale(reverse)
```

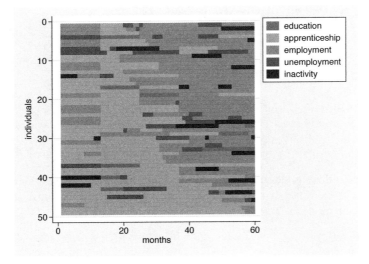

It is common to put personal identifiers on the *y*-axis, using the option `horizontal`, and put time on the *x*-axis.

In practice, with many individuals in a large panel, the bars become thinner lines. In such cases, you could use the plottype `rspike` instead. Note also that you can make room for more individuals by tuning the aspect ratio of the graph (see Cox 2004). There is no upper limit to how many individuals are shown, although as the number increases, the resulting graph may become too difficult to interpret. The readability, however, largely depends on how far similar individuals are grouped together. The sort order should therefore be some criterion of similarity between sequences.

To fine tune the graph, use any option allowed with `graph twoway`; type `help twoway_options`. Our example provides some simple illustrations. `legend()` changes the contents and placement of the legend. `xtitle()` defines the title along the *x*-axis. `ylabel()` is used to display the *y*-axis labels horizontally, instead of vertically. `yscale(reverse)` reverses the scale of the *y*-axis so that the first individual is plotted at the very top of the graph.

References

Brüderl, J., and S. Scherer. 2005, in press. Methoden zur Analyse von Sequenzdaten. *Kölner Zeitschrift für Soziologie und Sozialpsychologie* Sonderheft 44.

Cox, N. J. 2004. Stata tip 12: Tuning the plot region aspect ratio. *Stata Journal* 4: 357–358.

Scherer, S. 2001. Early career patterns: a comparison of Great Britain and West Germany. *European Sociological Review* 17: 119–144.

The Stata Journal (2005)
5, Number 4 , p. 604

Stata tip 26: Maximizing compatibility between Macintosh and Windows

Michael S. Hanson
Wesleyan University
mshanson@wesleyan.edu

A questioner on Statalist asked whether there are problems using Stata in a joint project on different operating systems. My short answer is "No". Underlying this is StataCorp's work to ensure that its official filetypes (`.dta`, `.gph`, `.ado`, `.do`, `.dct`, etc.) are completely compatible across all the operating systems it supports and that Stata can always read those files even from older versions.

My slightly longer answer is "Not with a few basic precautions", but much depends on how the collaboration occurs. Here is some advice for easier joint use of Stata across platforms (and indeed on the same platform).

Standardize Statas. Ideally, everyone should use the same version of Stata, with the same additional `.ado` files installed.

Avoid absolute file paths. (This strikes me as generally a good idea anyway, as it leads to greater portability.) If the project is sufficiently complex, create an identical subdirectory structure below some common project root directory on every file system and only use path references relative to this root.

Use forward slashes in file paths. Note that Stata understands the forward slash (/) as separating directory levels on all platforms, even Windows. So use that instead of the backward slash (\) for paths in all `.do` files.

Watch end-of-line delimiters. Text files have different line endings on Macintosh, Windows, and Unix systems. So long as users on different platforms are using sufficiently versatile text editors, it should be straightforward to read both input files (e.g., `.do` files) and output files (e.g., `.log` files) regardless of the line endings used—and, if necessary, to convert to the desired one. Note that how the files will be shared—common server, (s)FTP, email—may have implications for this issue.

Use Encapsulated PostScript. Save graphics in EPS format. (See the help or manual entry for `graph export`.) While the Macintosh can natively generate graphics in PDF format, the PC cannot (without jumping through some hoops and purchasing Acrobat, that is). WMF, EMF, and PICT do not translate well across platforms, and while you could use PNG, nonvector formats do not scale well. (As they are at a fixed size, when enlarged, they still contain only the lower-density information of the original, and when they are reduced, information must be lost to reduce their size.)

Use other open-standards file formats. More generally, collaboration will be easier if everyone uses open-standards file formats (e.g., plain text, PNG, TeX, or LaTeX, etc.)—instead of those tied to proprietary software.

The Stata Journal (2005)
5, Number 4 , pp. 605–607

Stata tip 27: Classifying data points on scatter plots

Nicholas J. Cox
Durham University
n.j.cox@durham.ac.uk

When you have scatter plots of counted or measured variables, you may often wish to classify data points according to the values of a further categorical variable. There are several ways to do this. Here we focus on the use of `separate`, gray-scale gradation, and text characters as class symbols. If different categories really do plot as distinct clusters, it should not matter too much how you show them, but knowing some Stata tricks should also help.

One starting point is that differing markers may be used on the plot whenever there are several variables plotted on the y-axis. With the `auto.dta` dataset, you can imagine

```
. sysuse auto
. gen mpg0 = mpg if foreign == 0
. gen mpg1 = mpg if foreign == 1
. scatter mpg? weight
```

Note the use of the wildcard `mpg?`, which picks up any variable names that have `mpg` followed by just one other character. Once the two variables `mpg0` and `mpg1` have been generated, different markers are automatic. This process still raises two questions. To get an acceptable graph, we need self-explanatory variable labels or at least self-explanatory text in the graph legend. Moreover, two categories are easy enough, but do we have to do this for each of say 5, 7, or 9 categories?

In fact, it would have been better to type

```
. separate mpg, by(foreign) veryshortlabel
. scatter mpg? weight
```

The command `separate` (see [D] **separate**) generates all the variables we need in one command and has a stab at labeling them intelligibly. In this case, we use the (undocumented) `veryshortlabel` option, which was implemented with graphics especially in mind. You may prefer the results of the documented `shortlabel` option. Note that the `by()` option can take true-or-false conditions, such as `price < 6000`, as well as categorical variables.

If your categorical variable consists of qualitatively different categories, you are likely to want to use qualitatively different symbols. Alternatively, if that variable is ordered or graded, the coding you use should also be ordered. One possibility is to use symbols colored in a sequence of gray scales.

Some data on landforms illustrate the point: Ian S. Evans kindly supplied measurements of 260 cirques in Wales, armchair-shaped hollows formerly occupied by small glaciers. Length tends to increase with width, approximately as a power function, but qualitative aspects of form, particularly how closely they approach a classic, well-developed shape, are also coded in a grade variable.

```
. separate length, by(grade) veryshortlabel
. scatter length? width, xsc(log) ysc(log) ms(O ..)
> mcolor(gs1 gs4 gs7 gs10 gs13) mlcolor(black ..) msize(*1.5 ..)
> yti("': variable label length'") yla(200 500 1000 2000, ang(h))
> xla(200 500 1000 2000) legend(pos(11) ring(0) col(1))
```

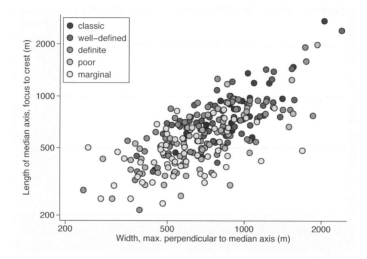

Figure 1 shows length versus width, subdivided by grade. Some practical details deserve emphasis. Gray scales near 16 (white) may be difficult to spot against a light background, including any printed page. Therefore, a dark outline color is recommended. Bigger symbols than the default are needed to do the coloring justice, but as a consequence, this approach is less likely to be useful with thousands of data points. A by() option showing different categories separately might work better. With the coding here, it so happens that the darkest category is plotted first and is thus liable to be overplotted by lighter categories wherever data points are dense. Some experimentation with the opposite order of plotting might be a good idea to see which works better.

An alternative that sometimes works nicely is to use ordinary text characters as different markers. One clean style is to suppress the marker symbols completely, using instead the contents of a `str1` variable as marker labels. Whittaker (1975, 224) gave data on net primary productivity and biomass density for various ecosystem types. Figure 2 shows the subdivision.

```
. scatter npp bd, xsc(log) ysc(log) ms(i) mlabpos(0) mlabsize(*1.4)
> mla(c) yla(3000 1000 300 100 30 10 3, nogrid ang(h))
> xla(0.01 "0.01" 0.1 "0.1" 1 10 100)
> legend(on ring(0) pos(5) order( - "m marine" - "w wet" - "c cultivated" -
> "g grassland" - "f forest" - "b bare"))
```

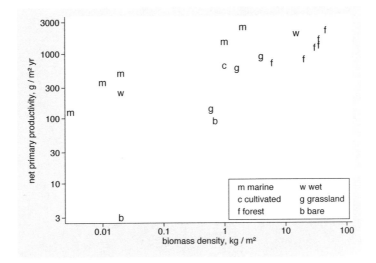

With three or four orders of magnitude variation in each variable, log scales are advisable. On those scales, there is a broad correlation whereby more biomass means higher productivity, but also considerable variation, much of which can be rationalized in terms of very different cover types. For the same biomass density, marine and other wet ecosystems have higher productivity than land ecosystems.

On the Stata side, remember `mlabpos(0)` and note that the `legend` must be set `on` explicitly. For different purposes, or for different tastes, what is here given as the legend might go better as text in a caption in a printed report. Behind the practice here lies general advice that lowercase letters, such as `abc`, work better than uppercase, such as `ABC`, as they are easier to distinguish from each other, and they are less likely to impart an synaesthetic sense in readers that the graph designer is shouting at them.

References

Whittaker, R. H. 1975. *Communities and Ecosystems*. New York: Macmillan.

The Stata Journal (2006)
6, Number 1 , pp. 144–146

Stata tip 28: Precise control of dataset sort order

L. Philip Schumm
Department of Health Studies
University of Chicago
Chicago, IL
pschumm@uchicago.edu

The observations in a Stata dataset are ordered, so that they may be referred to by their position (e.g., in 42/48) and that individual values of a variable may be referred to with subscripts (e.g., mpg[42]). This order can be changed by using the sort command (see [D] sort). Developing a full appreciation of what is possible using sort together with the by: prefix, the underscore built-ins _n and _N, and subscripting is a major step toward Stata enlightenment (e.g., see Cox [2002]).

One source of surprise for many users arises when sorting by one or more variables which, when taken together, do not uniquely determine the order of observations. In this case, the resulting order within any group of observations having the same value(s) of those variables is effectively random because sort uses an *unstable* sort algorithm. Users who desire a *stable* sort—in which the previous ordering of observations within tied values of the sort variables is maintained—should specify the stable option. However, this option will slow sort down and, more importantly, can hide problems in your code.

You are likely to discover this issue when coding an operation dependent on the order of the data that gives different results from one run to another. Consider the following dataset consisting of mothers and their children:

```
. list, sepby(family)
```

	family	name	child
1.	2	Harriet	0
2.	2	Lewis	1
3.	1	Sylvia	0
4.	1	Jenny	1
5.	3	Kim	0
6.	3	Peter	1
7.	3	Kim	1

Individuals are grouped by family, the mother always appearing first. Suppose that we want to construct a unique within-family identifier, such that all mothers have the same value. This is a straightforward application of by:, but first the data must be sorted by family:

```
. sort family
. by family: generate individual = _n
```

```
. table child individual

                 individual
       child        1     2     3

           0        2     1
           1        1     2     1
```

Unfortunately, the result is not as desired: one mother was assigned the value 2. In fact, following the call to `sort`, the order of observations within families—and hence the assignment of identifiers—was random. If we had instead sorted by family *and* child, each mother would have appeared first and would have been assigned a value of 1 (assuming that each family has exactly one mother—a key assumption that should always be checked). Yet even this solution would still be deficient: if a family has multiple children, their identifiers would be random and irreproducible. Only if we sort by family, child, *and* name would we have an adequate solution.

If we had used instead

```
. sort family, stable
```

we would also have obtained the desired result. So why does `sort` by default perform an unstable sort? Apart from better performance, the answer (emphasized by William Gould on Statalist) is that using the `stable` option not only fails to address the problem; it also reduces the chance of discovering it. Our error was to perform a calculation dependent on the sort order of the data without establishing that order beforehand. Using `stable` would have temporarily masked the error. However, had the sort order of the input dataset changed, we would have been in trouble.

How can you avoid such problems? First, train yourself to recognize when a calculation depends on the sort order of the data. Most instances in which you are using `_n` and `_N` or subscripting (either alone or with `by`) are easy to recognize. However, instances in which you are using a function that depends on the order of the data (e.g., `sum()` or `group()`) can be more subtle (Gould 2000).

Second, ensure that the order of the data is fully specified. This check became much easier in Stata 8 with the introduction of the `isid` command ([D] **isid**), which checks whether one or more variables uniquely identify the observations and returns an error if they do not. The command also has a `sort` option, which sorts the dataset in order of the specified variable(s). This option lets us replace our original `sort` command with

```
. isid family child name, sort
```

which, since it runs without error, confirms that we have specified the order fully. Had we used only `family`, or `family` and `child`, `isid` would have returned an error, immediately alerting us to the problem.

References

Cox, N. J. 2002. Speaking Stata: How to move step by: step. *Stata Journal* 2: 86–102.

Gould, W. 2000. FAQ: Sorting on categorical variables.
  http://www.stata.com/support/faqs/lang/sort.html.

The Stata Journal (2006)
6, Number 1 , pp. 146–148

Stata tip 29: For all times and all places

Charles H. Franklin
Department of Political Science
University of Wisconsin–Madison
Madison, WI
chfrankl@wisc.edu

According to the *Data Management Reference Manual*, the `cross` command is "rarely used"; see [D] **cross**. This comment understates the command's usefulness. For example, the `fillin` command uses `cross` (Cox 2005). Here is one further circumstance in which it proves extremely useful, allowing a simple solution to an otherwise awkward problem.

In pooled time-series cross-sectional data, we require that some number of units (geographic locations, patients, television markets) be observed over some period (daily from March to November, say). We thus need a data structure in which each unit is represented at each time point. If the data come in this complete form, then no problem arises. But when aggregating from lower-level observations, some dates, and possibly some units, are often missing. This missingness could be because no measurement was taken or because an event that is being counted simply did not occur on that date and so no record or observation was generated. In the aggregated Stata data file, no observation will appear for these dates or units. Inserting observations for the missing dates or units is awkward, but the `cross` command, followed by `merge`, makes the solution simple.

To illustrate with a real example: in the Wisconsin Advertising Project, we have coded 1.06 million political advertisements broadcast during the 2004 U.S. presidential campaign, using data provided by Nielsen Monitor-Plus. These ads are distributed across 210 media markets. Each time an ad is broadcast, it generates an observation in our dataset. The data are then aggregated to the media market to produce a daily count of the total advertising in each market. Such aggregation is simple in Stata. Variables `repad` and `demad` are coded 1 if the ad supported the Republican or Democratic candidate, respectively, and 0 otherwise. The sum is thus simply the count of the number of ads supporting each candidate.

```
clear
use allads
sort market date
collapse (sum) repad demad, by(market date) fast
save marketcounts, replace
```

This do-file produced no observation if no ads ran in a market on a particular date, which is common in these data. We want a dataset that includes every date for each of the 210 markets, with a value of 0 if no ad ran in a market on a date.

We can use `cross` to create a dataset that has one observation for each market for each of the 245 days included in our study. The file `dmacodelist.dta` contains one observation for each of the 210 markets: dma stands for "designated market area", Nielsen's term for television markets. First, we create a Stata dataset with 245 observations, one for each day of our study (March 3–November 2). Then we convert this information to a Stata date.

```
clear
set obs 245
gen date = _n + mdy(03,02,2004)
format date %d
```

Now use **cross** to generate the dataset with all dates for all markets:

```
cross using dmacodelist
sort market date
save alldates, replace
```

The file alldates.dta contains one observation for each market and for each date. The last step is to merge the aggregated marketcount.dta dataset with alldates.dta and replace missing values with zeros.

```
clear
use marketcounts
sort market date
merge market date using alldates
assert _merge != 1
replace demad = 0 if demad == .
replace repad = 0 if repad == .
```

The merge should produce no values of _merge that are 1, meaning observations found only in marketcounts, so the assert command checks this: the do-file will stop if the assertion is false (see Gould 2003 on assert). The repads and demads will be missing in the merged data only if no ad was broadcast, so replacing missing values for these variables with zeros will result in the desired dataset.

Thus the cross command offers an efficient solution to this type of problem. Those who often aggregate low-level data to create time-series cross-sectional structures will find this command handy.

References

Cox, N. J. 2005. Stata tip 17: Filling in the gaps. *Stata Journal* 5: 135–136.

Gould, W. 2003. Stata tip 3: How to be assertive. *Stata Journal* 3: 448.

The Stata Journal (2006)
6, Number 1 , pp. 149–150

Stata tip 30: May the source be with you

Nicholas J. Cox
Department of Geography
Durham University
Durham City, UK
n.j.cox@durham.ac.uk

Stata 9 introduced a command, `viewsource`, that does two things: it finds a text file along your ado-path and then opens the Viewer on that text file. See [P] **viewsource** and [U] **17.5 Where does Stata look for ado-files?** for the basic explanations. Naturally, if the text file does not exist as named, say, because you mistyped the name or because it really does not exist, you will get an error message.

Although intended primarily for Stata programmers, `viewsource` can be useful for examining (but not for editing) any text file you are working with. That can include program files, help files, text data files, do-files, log files, and other text documents. Binary or proprietary-format files are not banned, but the command is unlikely to be useful with them. The Viewer is, in particular, not a substitute for any word processor.

Here are some examples. A good way to learn about any Stata command defined by an ado-file is to look at the source code. You might be puzzled by some output, suspect a bug, or simply be curious. Even if you are not (yet) a Stata programmer, you can learn a lot by looking at the code. After all, it is just more Stata. Many, but not all, commands, generically *cmdname*, are defined by *cmdname*.`ado`—an ado-file with the same name as the command. The exceptions are part of the executable and not visible to you by using `viewsource` or indeed any other command. You might as well start reflexively:

```
. viewsource viewsource.ado
```

from which you will see that `viewsource`'s main actions are to (try to) find the file you specified using `findfile` and then to open the file using `view`. You will see other details too, and puzzling out what they do is a good exercise in program appreciation.

A second example is opening a help file. This action may seem redundant given the existence of the `help` command, but there is a noteworthy exception. `viewsource` fires up `view` with its `asis` option, so that interpreting the SMCL commands in any help file is disabled. This approach is useful for examining the SMCL producing the special markup effects that are evident when you use `help`. Suppose that you see code you want to emulate in your own help files. Then `viewsource` *cmdname*.`hlp` will show you how that was done, and you do not need to know exactly where the help file is on your machine, except that it must be on your ado-path. A useful template for producing help files is official Stata's `examplehelpfile.hlp`. Again, you do not need to know where it is, or to search for it, as `viewsource` will find it.

You do not need to be a Stata programmer, or even be interested in the innards of Stata programs or help files, to find `viewsource` useful. Other text files along your ado-path, which includes your current directory or folder, may be opened, too. However, do-files and log files are most likely to be in the current directory or folder, so just using `view` is more direct. Say that you want to repeat a successful but complicated `graph` command, which you carefully stored in a log file or do-file. Use `view` or `viewsource` and then search inside the Viewer using keywords to locate the command before copying it.

Note the emphasis on viewing. The Viewer is not an editor, so making changes to the file is not possible. Use the Viewer when you are clear that neither you nor others should be changing file content, even if the person in question has the requisite file permissions. That situation certainly applies to StataCorp-produced files. With colleagues and students who could do no end of damage if unchecked, this feature is invaluable. It is a limitation if you really do want to edit the file, but then you should already be thinking how to clone `viewsource` so that it fires up your favorite text editor (or Stata's own Do-file Editor). Variants on this idea already exist in Stataland, but writing your own editing command is a good early exercise for any budding Stata programmer.

The Stata Journal (2006)
6, Number 2 , pp. 279–280

Stata tip 31: Scalar or variable? The problem of ambiguous names

Gueorgui I. Kolev
Universitat Pompeu Fabra
Barcelona, Spain
gueorgui.kolev@upf.edu

Stata users often put numeric or string values into scalars, which is as easily done as

```
. scalar answer = 42
. scalar question = "What is the answer?"
```

The main discussion of scalars is in [P] **scalar**. Scalars can be used interactively or in programs and are faster and more accurate than local macros for holding values. This advantage would not matter with a number like 42, but it could easily matter with a number that was very small or very large.

Scalars have one major pitfall. It is documented in [P] **scalar**, but users are often bitten by it, so here is another warning. If a variable and a scalar have the same name, Stata always assumes that you mean the variable, not the scalar. This naming can apply even more strongly than you first guess: recall that variable names can be abbreviated so long as the abbreviation is unambiguous (see [U] **11.2 Abbreviation rules**).

Suppose that you are using the auto dataset:

```
. sysuse auto
(1978 Automobile Data)
. scalar p = 0.7
. display p
4099
```

What happened to 0.7? Nothing. It is still there:

```
. display scalar(p)
.7
. scalar list p
      p =            .7
```

What is the 4099 result? The dataset has a variable, `price`, and no other variable names begin with p, so p is understood to mean `price`. Moreover, `display` assumes that if you specify just a variable name, you want to see its value in the first observation, namely, `price[1]`. (The full explanation for that is another story.)

What should users do to be safe?

1. Use a different name. For example, you might introduce a personal convention about uppercase and lowercase. Many Stata users use only lowercase letters (and possibly numeric digits and underscores too) within variable names. Such users

could distinguish scalars by using at least one uppercase letter in their names. You could also use a prefix such as `sc_`, as in `sc_p`. If you forget your convention or if a user of your programs does not know about this convention, Stata cannot sense the interpretation you want. Thus this method is not totally safe.

2. Use the `scalar()` pseudofunction to spell out that you want a scalar. This method is totally safe, but some people find it awkward.

3. Use a temporary name for a scalar, as in

```
. tempname p
. scalar `p' = 0.7
```

Each scalar with a temporary name will be visible while the program in which it occurs is running and only in that program. Temporary names can be used interactively, too. (Your interactive session also counts for this purpose as a program.) In many ways, this method is the best solution, as it ensures that scalars can be seen only locally, which is usually better programming style.

The Stata Journal (2006)
6, Number 2 , p. 281

Stata tip 32: Do not stop

Stephen P. Jenkins
Institute for Social and Economic Research
University of Essex
Colchester, UK
stephenj@essex.ac.uk

The `do` command, for executing commands from a file, has one (and only one) option: `nostop`. As the online help file for `do` indicates, the option "allows the do-file to continue executing even if an error occurs. Normally, Stata stops executing the do-file when it detects an error (nonzero return code)."

This option can be useful in a variety of circumstances. For example,

1. You wish to apply, in a do-file, the same set of commands to data referring to different groups of subjects or different periods. The commands for each dataset might fail with an error because, say, there are no relevant observations or an `ml` problem may not converge. Running the do-file with the `nostop` option will allow you to get the desired results for all datasets that do not produce an error and, at the same time, identify the potential source of error in the others. The `nostop` option is most useful in initial analyses. Error sources in particular datasets, once identified, can be trapped by using `capture`; if necessary, alternative action may be taken.

2. You have written a command and want to produce a script certifying that using incorrect syntax leads to an appropriate error. There may be several options and several ways in which syntax may be incorrect. With `nostop`, you can test that each of many incorrectly specified options works as expected, while having the do-file containing the test commands run to completion.

The Stata Journal (2006)
6, Number 2 , pp. 282–283

Stata tip 33: Sweet sixteen: Hexadecimal formats and precision problems

Nicholas J. Cox
Department of Geography
Durham University
Durham City, UK
n.j.cox@durham.ac.uk

Computer users generally supply numeric inputs as decimals and expect numerical outputs as decimals. But underneath the mapping from inputs to outputs lies software (such as Stata) and hardware that are really working with binary representations of those decimals. Much ingenuity goes into ensuring that conversions between decimal and binary are invisible to you, but occasionally you may see apparently strange side effects of this fact. This problem is documented in [U] **13.10 Precision and problems therein**, but it still often bites and puzzles Stata users. This tip emphasizes that the special hexadecimal format %21x can be useful in understanding what is happening. The format is also documented, but in just one place, [U] **12.5.1 Numeric formats**. Decimal formats such as %23.18f can also be helpful for investigating precision problems.

Binary representations of numbers, using just the two digits 0 and 1, can be difficult for people to interpret without extra calculations. The great advantage of a hexadecimal format, using base 16 (i.e., 2^4), is that it is closer to base 10 representations while remaining truthful about what can be held in memory as a representation of a number. It is conventional to use the decimal digits 0–9 and the extra digits a–f when base 16 is used. Thus a represents 10 and f represents 15. Hence, at its simplest, hexadecimal 10 represents decimal 16, hexadecimal 11 represents decimal 17, and so forth. (Think of 11 as $1 \times 16^1 + 1 \times 16^0$, for example.) In practice, we want to hold fractions and, as far as possible, some extremely large and extremely small numbers. The general format of a hexadecimally represented number in Stata is thus mXp, to be read as $m \times 2^p$. Thus if you use the format %21x with display, you can see examples:

```
. di %21x 1
+1.0000000000000X+000
. di %21x -16
-1.0000000000000X+004
. di %21x 1/16
+1.0000000000000X-004
```

You see that 1, -16, and 1/16 are, respectively, 1×2^0, -1×2^4, and 1×2^{-4}.

The special format is useful to others besides the numerical analysts mentioned in [U] **12.5.1 Numeric formats**. If you encounter puzzling results, looking at the numbers in question should help clarify what Stata is doing and why it does not match your expectation.

Users get bitten in two main ways. First, they forget that most of the decimal digits .1, .2, .3, .4, .5, .6, .7, .8, and .9 cannot be held exactly. Of these, only .5 (1/2) can possibly be represented exactly by a binary approximation; all the others must be held approximately only—regardless of how many bytes are used. To convince yourself of this, see that, e.g., 42.5 can be held exactly,

```
. di %21x 42.5
+1.5400000000000X+005
. di (1 + 5/16 + 4/256) * 2^5
42.5
```

whereas 42.1 cannot be held exactly,

```
. di %21x 42.1
+1.50ccccccccccdX+005
. di %23.18f 42.1
  42.100000000000001421
```

Close, but not exact. Second, users forget that although very large or very small numbers can be held approximately, not all possible numbers can be distinguished, even when those numbers are integers within the limits of the variable type being used.

A common source of misery is trying to hold nine-digit integers in numeric variables. If these are identifiers, holding them as str9 variables is a good idea, but let us focus on what often happens when users read such integers into numeric variables. This experiment shows the problems that can ensue.

```
. gen pinid = 123456789
. di %9.0f pinid[1]
123456792
. di %21x pinid[1]
+1.d6f3460000000X+01a
```

Stata did not complain, but it did not oblige. The value is off by 3. You will see that the value held is a multiple of 4, as the last two digits 92 are divisible by 4. Did we or Stata do something stupid? Can we fix it?

```
. replace pinid = pinid - 3
(0 real changes made)
```

Trying to subtract 3 gives us the same number, so far as Stata is concerned. What is going on? By default, Stata is using a float variable. See [D] **data types** if you want more information. At this size of number, such a variable can hold only multiples of 4 exactly, so we lose many final digits. The remedy, if a numeric variable is needed, is to use a long or double storage type instead.

Subscribe to the Stata Journal

Subscriptions are available from StataCorp, 4905 Lakeway Drive, College Station, Texas 77845, telephone 979-696-4600 or 800-STATA-PC, fax 979-696-4601, or online at

http://www.stata.com/bookstore/sj.html

Subscription rates:

Subscriptions mailed to U.S. and Canadian addresses:

3-year subscription (includes printed and electronic copy)	$165
2-year subscription (includes printed and electronic copy)	$115
1-year subscription (includes printed and electronic copy)	$ 59
1-year student subscription (includes printed and electronic copy)	$ 35
1-year university library subscription (includes printed and electronic copy)	$ 75
1-year institutional subscription (includes printed and electronic copy)	$175

Subscriptions mailed to other countries:

3-year subscription (includes printed and electronic copy)	$240
2-year subscription (includes printed and electronic copy)	$165
1-year subscription (includes printed and electronic copy)	$ 84
3-year subscription (electronic only)	$160
1-year student subscription (includes printed and electronic copy)	$ 59
1-year university library subscription (includes printed and electronic copy)	$ 95
1-year institutional subscription (includes printed and electronic copy)	$195

Back issues of the *Stata Journal* may be ordered online at

http://www.stata.com/bookstore/sj.html

The *Stata Journal* is published quarterly by the Stata Press, College Station, Texas, USA.